Walking With Abba Father

Walking With Abba Father

Six Psalms that Reveal God's Heart for You

DONDI DUELL

ISBN: 979-8-89694-221-4 - eBook

ISBN: 979-8-89694-222-1 - Paperback

Dedicated to my children and grandchildren, both here and yet to come. May the Lord bless you and fill you with his love to overflowing, and may you know him intimately as your Abba Father.

Table of Contents

Introduction

Enjoying the Journey
with Abba Father

We've all heard the saying, "Enjoy the journey," which tells us to embrace the process of learning and growing, even if we make mistakes along the way. But for me, enjoying the journey has always been easier said than done. For many years, I was afraid to slip up. I was afraid of being judged for not "doing the journey" perfectly. This fear gave me a view of life that was scary and harsh, and so I was not enjoying my journey.

I've since learned that if you do your faith journey with a loving God, he covers all your mistakes and lovingly teaches you. Your journey *does* become enjoyable. God's love is truly amazing, and his love set me free from that fear of making mistakes. Growing my faith was a process, and it was not achieved by being good and following the rules. My faith grew when I believed that God loved and cared about me.

When I was seventeen years old, I set aside some time to seek God because I wanted to know him better. I decided to pray, and as I was praying, I heard the word *Abba* in my mind. I spoke the word aloud but had no idea what it meant. My prayer time ended, and I felt I had not connected with God. A few days later, I found out *Abba* was the Hebrew word for "daddy." That blew my mind! I realized then that God had spoken his name—Abba—to me and invited me to know him as my loving Abba Father. This was very special to me.

I believe God invites each one of us to know him as our loving Abba Father. Later in my life, I discovered this verse: "Because you are sons [and daughters], God has sent forth the Spirit of His Son into our hearts, crying out, 'Abba! Father!'" (Galatians 4:6). Amazing! The Spirit of God causes our hearts to call our heavenly Father "Abba Father." Hebrew-speaking children still use this word today to address their own dads. *Abba* means "father," but its connotation is intimate—it's better translated as "daddy." When we use the name *Abba* in reference to God, we express personal intimacy with God and a spirit of sonship. How wonderful that the Spirit of God causes our hearts to desire relationship with our heavenly Father and to know him as our loving Abba!

For some years, as I journeyed with Abba Father, I found myself visualizing him on a throne and me coming into his throne room with my requests. Even though I knew he loved me, it felt a little daunting to go before him. One day, I could tell Abba Father wanted to change something. As I sat with him, he changed my mental image—instead of a throne, I found myself imagining a couch. He was sitting on the couch and invited me to sit with him—like a kind, loving father would.

Abba Father is a loving father who wants to spend time with you, to pour his love over you, to tell you he is proud of you, to give you good gifts, and to provide for you. What a neat father! Drawing close to him allows us to rejoice: "O taste and see that the Lord is good; how blessed is the man who takes refuge in Him!" (Psalm 34:8).

This book will take us on a faith journey through six psalms and show us that Abba Father promises us his love, his presence, and a place of refuge. For me, walking with Abba Father through these six psalms was pivotal to renewing and healing my heart deep down. As I have meditated on these psalms, my life has changed from one of brokenness, fear, and timidity to one of restoration, love, and confidence that Abba Father loves me as his daughter. It was like Abba brought me back to life through his Word and his presence. These psalms gave me a new realization of Abba Father's love for me and his nearness to me. I learned how to have faith in him and how to walk with him through both the easy and hard events of life. Abba brought me each psalm in its season, and I meditated on that psalm until he brought me another psalm. I learned so much about his character by meditating on each psalm.

Your relationship with Abba is a living, dynamic relationship, and he wants to show his goodness to you. You can make room to taste and see for yourself that he is good. We taste with our experience and with our emotions. As you spend time with Abba Father, you will find a closer, deeper relationship with him, and you will be blessed. As you experience life with Abba, you will become better at seeing his goodness toward you and believing in his love for you. As you get to know Abba Father, you will begin to see yourself the way Abba sees you—as a treasured son or daughter: "Then you will call on me and come and pray to me, and I will listen to you. You will seek me and find me when you seek me with all your heart" (Jeremiah 29:12–13, NIV).

Abba desires a relationship with you. When you pray to him, he will listen to you. When you seek him, you will find him. Abba loves you that much! In the book of Zephaniah, we read:

> The Lord your God in your midst,
> The Mighty One, will save;
> He will rejoice over you with gladness,
> He will quiet you with His love,
> He will rejoice over you with singing.
> (Zephaniah 3:17, NKJV)

This verse says Abba Father comes to be with you and to calm you with his love. He is not coming to condemn you but to save you. He gives you his peace and rejoices that you are his son or daughter by singing over you. Abba Father *likes* you. He is inviting you into a closer relationship with him. This relationship is a way of living where you believe you are Abba Father's favorite and he will hear your prayers and answer you. This is a relationship I have experienced and am so thankful for. The more I believe verses like Zephaniah 3:17, the more I trust Abba. The more I trust Abba, the more confidently I pray, certain that he cares about what I care about (see 1 Peter 5:7).

Reflecting on these psalms has been a wonderful experience for me. It has allowed me to "sit on the couch" with Abba

Father and become acquainted with his goodness. He has become someone I can rely on. He will become someone you can rely on too!

HOW TO USE THIS BOOK

Each chapter in this book will start with a psalm to read and have a key point that reveals an aspect of Abba Father's nature. Each chapter will reflect on the psalm and key point to learn what Abba Father is revealing about himself.

At the end of every chapter, in the sections titled *Activation* and *Recharge*, there will be an opportunity to spend time with Abba Father and receive his love for you. The Activation sections provide chapter-specific considerations to bring with you into the Recharge sections, which are meant to fill up your spirit (think of recharging a phone battery!). Our spirit, soul, and body need recharging, and Abba Father is the living God who can fill us with love and acceptance, joy and peace, purpose and direction, and health and wholeness. Recharging at the end of every chapter should take you at least ten minutes, though you should feel free to linger as you are able. The time will be divided into (1) sitting with Abba Father in silence, (2) reading Psalm 126 and the psalm for the coming chapter, (3) journaling, and (4) ending your time with Abba Father in silence again. The times provided in the Recharge section are recommendations, not limitations. Consider using a timer to free yourself from keeping track of the minutes on your own.

I recommend doing each chapter's Recharge portion for at least four days before moving on to the next chapter in the book. This will give Abba Father a chance to speak to your heart about the psalm and highlight his love for you. Each day you recharge, you will receive something new from Abba Father.

Listening to instrumental music is very helpful to me when I recharge. The music minimizes distractions and helps me focus since it has no words. I like listening to *Instrumental Soaking Worship* music for my recharge moments with Abba. For other times during the day, I like listening to worship music with words. So, in each Recharge section, I list a few of Mack Brock's songs as a resource for you. Mack Brock is a wonderful worship leader, and his songs have been a key part of me being able to keep my eyes on Abba Father and his promises. I highly recommend listening to Mack Brock's songs as you have time—while getting ready in the morning, while driving, in the evening, or whenever there is space. Mack Brock's songs are full of praise, worship, Scripture, and healing, and they will help guard your heart and your mind.

This book is meant for individual study but can easily be used in a group setting. In a group setting, the Recharge times can still be done individually. At each meeting, before starting the next chapter, group members can share with each other what Abba Father has revealed in their time with him. Sharing together will make studying the chapter richer. Discussing a chapter and sharing in a group setting will take sixty to ninety minutes.

I'm excited you are here reading this book, and I'm excited for what Abba Father is going to do in your life through these chapters. These psalms will show you that Abba Father is walking with you and that you are not alone. Abba loves you so much and delights in you. Receiving Abba Father's love for you is key to healing your heart and growing your faith. Together we will anchor ourselves in Abba Father's love for us and in our identity as his sons and daughters. You are important to Abba, he loves you, and he will never leave you. Abba Father is so good, and this will be fun!

Chapter 1

The Promise

Psalm 126

¹ When the LORD brought back the captive
ones of Zion,
we were like those who dream.
² Then our mouth was filled with laughter,
and our tongue with joyful shouting;
Then they said among the nations,
"The LORD has done great things for them."
³ The LORD has done great things for us;
We are glad.
⁴ Restore our captivity, O LORD,
as the streams in the South.
⁵ Those who sow with tears
will reap with joyful shouting.
⁶ He who goes to and fro weeping,

carrying his bag of seed,
will indeed come again with a shout of joy,
bringing his sheaves with him.

Psalm 126 is about the restoration of the Israelites from
captivity in Babylon back to their home in Jerusalem, or
Zion as they sometimes called it. The father of the Israelites
was Abraham, and all his descendants were called *Israelites*.
Gentile refers to people who are not Israelites. Why does this
matter? Abraham set the standard for faith by believing in
God's promises to him. Galatians explains that if people are
believers in Jesus Christ, they will be included in the family of
Abraham and be heirs of Abraham, even if they are Gentiles:

> Even so Abraham believed God, and it was
> reckoned to him as righteousness. Therefore,
> be sure that it is those who are of faith who are
> sons of Abraham. The Scripture, foreseeing
> that God would justify the Gentiles by faith,
> preached the gospel beforehand to Abraham,
> *saying*, "All the nations will be blessed in you."
> So then those who are of faith are blessed
> with Abraham, the believer. . . . And if you
> belong to Christ, then you are Abraham's
> descendants, heirs according to promise.
> (Galatians 3:6–9, 29)

Whoever has put their faith in Jesus Christ for their salvation
is blessed with Abraham and one of Abraham's heirs. We are
included in the promises of Psalm 126. This psalm, then,
is also about Abba Father restoring us from captivity and

bringing us back to our original design that he intended for us.

Before we continue, I invite you to reread Psalm 126 with fresh eyes. As you read, consider what Abba Father is promising you and the impact of these verses.

I have heard people speak of holding on to God's promise for them, and I have asked myself, "How did that person get a promise from God? How do *I* get a promise from God?" Years later, when I realized that I was holding on to Psalm 126 as God's promise to me, I asked Abba Father, "How do other people get promises from you that they can hold on to?"

I heard Abba Father say, "Psalm 126 can be for them too." So yes! These promises in Psalm 126 are for me, and they are for you. Take these promises and hold them tight, as instructed in 2 Corinthians: "For no matter how many promises God has made, they are 'Yes' in Christ. And so, through Him the 'Amen' is spoken by us to the glory of God" (2 Corinthians 1:20, NIV).

All of Abba's promises are for us. Abba Father gives us promises, and Jesus says "yes" to these promises. Our job is to agree with Jesus and speak this agreement out loud. By believing in Abba's promises to us and saying these promises out loud to ourselves, we are speaking our "amen" and glorifying God.

ABBA FATHER'S PROMISE OF RESCUE AND OUR RESPONSE

Psalm 126 is a chapter full of promises of rescue and restoration, of joy and fulfillment, and of sorrows that will yield fruit as we are faithful. These promises speak of Abba Father's goodness to us throughout our life. Let's look at these promises:

> When the LORD brought back the captive
> ones of Zion,
> we were like those who dream.
> Then our mouth was filled with laughter,
> and our tongue with joyful shouting;
> Then they said among the nations,
> "The LORD has done great things for them."
> The LORD has done great things for us;
> We are glad. (Psalm 126:1–3)

The first half of Psalm 126 speaks about the amazing rescue and restoration Abba Father has for us and our response to him. These are such fun verses, full of laughter and joy. It reads like the happy ending of a long story. While he will do great things for us at the end of our story, Abba Father is also working right now, in the middle of our story. He is already at work in our lives. Our rescue from captivity is for both now and for the future. Our rescue is certain.

I can see now that Abba brought me to different moments of freedom from captivity throughout my life in wonderful ways. The first time I read these verses, I was about seventeen. I grabbed on to the joy and said, "Yes, Lord! This is awesome!"

But I didn't fully understand what the verses meant. It wasn't until a few years later that Abba brought me my first rescue. I was twenty years old, and Abba freed me from fear of relationship. I was praying with an older couple, and Abba revealed to them that I had resolved in my heart not to trust men. They prayed the simplest prayer I'd ever heard to renounce that distrust in Jesus's name, and I was instantly set free. After this prayer, I could easily interact with men, and I felt free. I was no longer afraid in conversations with them, and I felt peace. It was so easy for Abba to do, and my life was forever changed.

Another time, in my thirties, Abba freed me from the fear of fully trusting him with my physical and emotional well-being. I had a friend who shared with me how God was teaching her to trust him. I remember thinking I trusted God to take care of other people, but I was not sure I had faith to believe he would take care of me. I didn't want God to know my thoughts, and then the realization hit me that God knew all my thoughts already. This was both funny and troubling to me, and it revealed I was still trying to earn God's love by being good. I'm sure that made Abba Father laugh. He was so gentle with me and taught me how to trust him with the things that are important to me whether physical or emotional. He has proven himself to be trustworthy throughout my life.

After that, Abba taught me to let go of offenses by choosing to forgive others. This was hard at first, but the freedom Abba brought me when I forgave both small and big offenses made it totally worth it. Throughout my life, Abba has taught me to know him and to believe in him.

Abba Father is so good. Each time Abba has set me free, I have been amazed and felt like I was dreaming, as Psalm 126:1 says. Over the years, I have happened upon Psalm 126 and reignited my faith that Abba Father is promising to be good to me. As we know, the events of life are not all laughter and joy. Some are hard and disappointing. Now, I can look back over my life and see Abba's goodness to me and his nearness even in the hard and disappointing times. Sometimes in the middle of life, we can only see what is right in front of us. Abba Father can see it all; he knows our lives in their entirety, from beginning to end. He will rescue us as we journey, and he calls us to *believe* in his rescue and in his goodness to us. He calls us to faith: "Now faith is the assurance of things hoped for, the conviction of things not seen" (Hebrews 11:1).

Faith is being sure that Abba will accomplish what He has promised to us. Conviction is something you don't waver from. Abba Father asks us to have conviction that he will accomplish what we cannot see now.

Think of a situation where you currently need rescue. Say out loud to Abba right now, "I believe that you will accomplish what you have promised me. I believe you are with me right now and you will rescue me from captivity." Now we choose to look past our current circumstances into our future and anticipate all the good he has planned for us. If you do this, it is called *faith*. Our faith pleases Abba (see Hebrews 11:2).

Nehemiah assures us, "And do not be worried, for the joy of the Lord is your strength and your stronghold" (Nehemiah 8:10, AMP). I once wrongly assumed this verse was saying that if I had joy, then I would be strengthened, but I have never really known how to get joy in the middle of everything. But this verse says that Abba's joy is the very thing that strengthens us—the joy of the Lord is *itself* our strength! You can be strengthened by Abba's joy. Abba is full of joy because he sees the good he has planned for you here and now *and* in your future. Abba invites you to see what he sees. When you look past your circumstances into your future to the fulfillment of his promise, then Abba Father's joy becomes your joy today, right in the middle of your circumstances. You start seeing what Abba sees and are filled with hope and joy. The joy of the Lord gives you strength to keep walking and believing in him. It gives you a new perspective filled with joy. Walking with Abba Father gives us access to this joy that strengthens us.

This is where verse two of Psalm 126 is activated: "Then our mouth was filled with laughter and our tongue with joyful shouting; then they said among the nations, 'The LORD has done great things for them.'" Our mouth is filled with laughter because we have begun to interact with Abba's goodness to us. Our speech is full of joy because we know Abba is taking care of us. Others see our joy and declare Abba has done great things for us. Let me repeat this: *Others will see our joy and declare Abba has done great things for us.* They will see Abba has blessed us and set us free, and they will be drawn to Jesus. This is amazing. Abba brings us true freedom as we interact with his goodness. Abba Father is so good, and we get to declare it and be glad (see Psalm 126:3).

THE JOURNEY AND THE PROMISE OF FRUIT

> Restore our captivity, O LORD,
> as the streams in the South.
> Those who sow with tears
> will reap with joyful shouting.
> He who goes to and fro weeping,
> carrying his bag of seed,
> will indeed come again with a shout of joy,
> bringing his sheaves with him.
> (Psalm 126:4–6)

The second half of Psalm 126 speaks about the journey of our life and Abba Father's promise of our restoration. There is also a promise of fruit that will come from our sorrow as we are faithful to walk with Abba.

When I read these verses for myself and considered what they meant, I felt like they were hard verses full of weeping and sadness. I did not like them at all. As I wrestled with Abba Father about whether he was keeping up his part to restore my life, I told him that he was not enough and that I needed my relationships restored for me to be happy. I felt empty and not full of joy. I felt alone. I am so thankful that Abba is okay with us being honest with him. Abba Father already knows our thoughts, and he sees down into the depths of our heart. As I mentioned above, we can't hide our thoughts from God—we are only hiding them from ourselves. Abba loves it when we are honest with him, and his goal is to heal our heart and to love us completely, causing us to love him.

As I was faithful to journey with Abba Father through Psalm 126, I realized that my heart had changed and drawn close to him. I realized that he had done so much more in my life than I could have ever wanted. Most importantly, I realized that being with Abba really *was* enough. I realized that my great prize was having a relationship with Abba, and this was more valuable to me than having my other relationships restored. I saw that Abba had been loving me back to wholeness. My life had not changed into all that I wanted, yet I was content; I felt safe and knew Abba Father loved me so much.

Here are some promises I've learned from reading and rereading Psalm 126:

- Abba will free me from what I am in captivity to.
- Abba will restore me and bring me back to my original design.
- Abba will do more than I can think or imagine; it will be like I am dreaming.
- Abba will restore my joy.
- Abba walks with me.
- Abba sees my tears.
- Abba will make rivers flow in my desert places.
- Abba will bring joy from my heartache, more than I can hold.
- Abba will bring fruit out of my faithfulness, more than I can carry.

Now, when I read Psalm 126:4–6, I feel seen by Abba. He sees my tears and cares about me. I can see his hand directing my life and know he has always been with me. Now I can interact with Abba in hope for my future, knowing that he has good planned for me. I look for his solutions and can trust in his timing. We don't know how Abba Father is going to restore us, but his timing will likely be very different from our timetable. I can with confidence tell you that his way is the best way and covers more than we could anticipate. Ultimately, I get to walk in peace and joy that comes from him as he directs my steps.

Abba's promise to restore our joy is for now. I need his joy in my current situation, not just in my future. I need Abba to refresh me daily. I need Abba's perspective throughout my day. When you walk with Abba Father, you will have your joy restored and find a wonderful relationship with him. You can pray, "Come now and restore me. Your way is good. Make streams in the dryness. Refresh me."

Abba Father says he will never leave us or forsake us, but there have still been moments in my life where I felt betrayed and abandoned by him. In those moments, I continued soaking in these psalms by memorizing them and rehearsing the verses in my mind. I allowed their truths to wash and renew my mind. I allowed Abba to give me his perspective and restore my hope. I allowed Abba Father to minister to my heart by just sitting with him in silence. He has been faithful to stay with me and never leave.

Our heavenly Father sees you and your tears. He will not leave you or forsake you. He wants to minister to your heart and restore your hope and your joy. Abba is so good. Abba is offering to walk with you through the hard times and the good times, and verses 5 and 6 say there will be fruit that comes from your life when you allow Abba to walk with you. Part of that fruit is your testimony, which will impact others by urging them to turn to Abba Father and believe in Jesus. This is truly something to shout joyfully about!

This journey you are on is worthwhile because of Abba's promise of his presence, his restoration, and his joy for you. Hold these promises tight to your heart. Abba Father has made provision for you to go beyond just a bearable life—you are meant to live a thriving life. Whether you walk with Abba or not, you will still have to walk your journey. You can choose to walk with Abba Father or ignore him, but Abba Father doesn't leave you. As Psalm 34:8 reminds us, you are blessed when you take refuge in Abba and walk with him: "O taste and see that the Lord is good; how blessed is the man who takes refuge in Him!"

Abba Father will interact with you in love, happiness, and acceptance, and you will get better and better at hearing Abba's love messages to you.

As we prepare for this chapter's Activation, let's remember:

1. Abba loves it when you have faith and believe in Him (see Hebrews 11:1–2).
2. Abba looks at you with love and is so happy with you (see Zephaniah 3:17).
3. Abba will hear your prayers, and He will answer you (see Jeremiah 29:12–13).

Abba Father is good.

ACTIVATION

If our faith journey needs a relationship with Abba Father, then our relationship will need to be cultivated. I have found sitting with Abba for even a few minutes to be very effective. I like to have instrumental soaking worship music playing so that I am not distracted as I sit with Abba. During the first few minutes, I don't pray or worship or intercede while I am sitting with Abba. Rather I'm in a posture of being present and listening. I just sit with Abba and enjoy his presence. He might speak to me or give me a picture, or he may just let me sit surrounded by his love. If my thoughts wander, I try to see if Abba is leading my thoughts and then interact with him about my thoughts.

The following Recharge section will give you a framework for cultivating your relationship with Abba Father in a new way. The main goal of the Recharge section is to connect with Abba's love for you. The second goal is to hear from Abba. Two points I want to make:

1. We need to be recharged with love from Abba just as Jesus was, as he says in John 15:9: "Just as the Father has loved Me, I have also loved you; abide in My love."
2. You can have an expectation that Abba will speak to you. In John 10:27, Jesus tells us, "My sheep hear My voice, and I know them, and they follow Me."

The Recharge section will include reading Psalm 16 before reading the next chapter in this book. This will allow you to connect with Abba and allow him to speak to your heart about Psalm 16 before we cover it in Chapter 2. Abba will tell you the things he wants you to know. You can spend as many days as you want recharging with Abba and reading Psalm 16. I recommend spending at least four days recharging before moving on to Chapter 2. We will also keep Psalm 126 in front of us throughout this book since this is our anchor promise. Enjoy recharging with Abba Father!

RECHARGE WITH ABBA FATHER

Total time: 10–15 minutes

While not required, you may use a timer to structure your time. The framework offered below is for a ten-minute Recharge time, but you are invited to extend this time to fifteen minutes or longer. This ten to fifteen minutes is where you can listen to instrumental soaking worship music if you like.

Minutes 1–3: Silence and Reflection

The Recharge time will begin and end with a few minutes sitting with Abba. To begin, recite the phrase from Psalm 46:10, "Be still and know that I am God." Shorten the phrase each time to set your heart. Notice the nuances of shortening the phrase:

> *Be still and know that I am God.*
> *Be still and know that I am.*
> *Be still and know.*
> *Be still.*
> *Be.*

For the remainder of the three minutes, sit in silence with Abba Father and just be with him. This might feel uncomfortable at first, but as you get to know Abba and his heart of love toward you, you will become more comfortable sitting in silence and being loved by him. At the end, write down anything you have seen, sensed, or heard spoken to you. Know that it is okay and normal if you do not see or sense or hear anything. Abba enjoys simply being with you.

Minutes 3–5: Reading

Read Psalm 126; then read Psalm 16.

Minutes 5–8: Journaling

Write down any verses from these psalms Abba Father has highlighted and their meaning to you. This will allow you to remember what Abba has spoken to your heart.

Minutes 8–10: Sitting with Abba

End your time by spending two minutes in silence with Abba Father. At the end, write down anything you have seen, sensed, or heard spoken to you.

Throughout your day:

Worship songs to listen to throughout your day: "I Am Loved" by Mack Brock, "Greater Things" by Mack Brock, "Covered" by Mack Brock, "Bless the One" by Mack Brock

Chapter 2

The Prayer

Psalm 16

[1] Preserve me, O God, for I take refuge in You.
[2] I said to the LORD, "You are my Lord;
I have no good besides You."
[3] As for the saints who are in the earth,
They are the majestic ones in whom is all my delight.
[4] The sorrows of those who have bartered for another god will be multiplied;
I shall not pour out their drink offerings of blood,
Nor will I take their names upon my lips.
[5] The LORD is the portion of my inheritance and my cup;
You support my lot.

⁶ The lines have fallen to me in pleasant places;
Indeed, my heritage is beautiful to me.
⁷ I will bless the LORD who has counseled me;
Indeed, my mind instructs me in the night.
⁸ I have set the LORD continually before me;
Because He is at my right hand, I will not be shaken.
⁹ Therefore my heart is glad and my glory rejoices;
My flesh also will dwell securely.
¹⁰ For You will not abandon my soul to Sheol;
Nor will You allow Your Holy One to undergo decay.
¹¹ You will make known to me the path of life;
In Your presence is fullness of joy;
In Your right hand there are pleasures forever.

Psalm 16 is a wonderful prayer that gives us insight into how to position ourselves before Abba Father. Psalm 16 is also packed full of promises that will sustain us and teach us Abba Father is for us.

Our Abba Father is oriented toward our good. Abba is for us and not against us. When we believe Abba is for us, we will begin to think differently and trust him more. As we spend time with Abba, we lean into these verses from Psalm 16. I describe "leaning" as putting our trust in something, as we see in Proverbs 3:5: "Trust in the Lord with all your heart and do not lean on your own understanding." We are instructed to lean on Abba Father, not our own thinking. I trust in these verses from Psalm 16. When I run to Abba daily for him to flood me with new life, I get to know his nature and character. He is so good and kind and faithful. The important thing is for us to experience Abba's goodness and kindness and faithfulness for ourselves. In Psalm 16 we will see our need for Abba, our position as his beloved children, and Abba's provision for us. We will see that Abba is for us.

OUR NEED FOR ABBA

> Preserve me, O God, for I take refuge in You.
> I said to the LORD, "You are my Lord;
> I have no good besides You."
> As for the saints who are in the earth,
> They are the majestic ones in whom is all my delight.
> The sorrows of those who have bartered for another god will be multiplied;
> I shall not pour out their drink offerings of blood,
> Nor will I take their names upon my lips.
> (Psalm 16:1–4)

Our ultimate need is to be in relationship with Abba. These verses give us a lens with which to view Abba and direct our thoughts. Abba is walking with us and does not leave us, no matter what we do or what happens. Abba loves us. Acknowledging our need of Abba and his goodness to us is key to setting our heart in the right posture in prayer.

Abba highlights four of our needs in this passage:

1. We need Abba Father to preserve our life (verse 1).
2. We need Abba Father to be Lord of our life (verse 2).
3. We need other believers in our life (verse 3).
4. We need Abba Father to show us our heart (verse 4).

In short, we need Abba. Abba loves us and is for us. When we believe Abba Father is for us, we will be able to turn to him for help and trust in him. Let's look at these four needs in detail.

We Need Abba Father to Preserve Our Life

"Preserve me, O God, for I take refuge in You" (Psalm 16:1). What does it look like for Abba to preserve our life? When life is stressful, we can turn to Abba as our source of peace, and we will be kept preserved and whole. We can leave the details to him, knowing that he cares and has our good in mind, as well as the wisdom to accomplish the best outcome.

One day, I could feel my stress increasing all morning as I knew I had a lunch date that had the potential to be full of conflict. My imagination was going wild imagining everything that could go wrong. I decided to stop and sit in Abba's presence for a few minutes. He filled me with his peace, and I was able to stop my mind from partnering with all the negative thoughts. This brought me back to the truth that Abba was near. He would be with me at lunch and direct my conversation. I was able to walk in his peace and not partner with fear. I could trust in Abba's presence.

Likewise, you can also turn to Abba in the middle of your day. Allow Abba to interact with you and minister to your heart. He knows everything and is already planning to help you. He will preserve your life.

We Need Abba Father to Be Lord of Our Life

Verse two of Psalm 16 says, "I said to the LORD, 'You are my Lord; I have no good besides You.'" Abba thinks differently than we do, and Scripture says that his decisions are more wonderful than what we could ask or think (see Ephesians 3:20). If this is true, then I want Abba Father to be Lord of my life. If Abba is going to be Lord of my life, then I will need to upgrade my thoughts to his thoughts and my perspective to his perspective.

I have had to upgrade my perspective to Abba's perspective in most of my thinking. Naturally, I find myself thinking of my own desires and about what is not going according to my plan. This leads me to judge others and to be critical. This old way of thinking will hurt me in time. I've learned to listen to my thoughts and recognize that the negative ones are not from Abba. His thoughts about situations are from the perspective of life and love, and they always have the end in mind. He sees the good he has planned and knows the best way to achieve life and love in my heart. I want to think like him, and I choose to believe him.

One of my strategies for adopting Abba's perspective is to say out loud the opposite of what I'm thinking. This helps orient my heart back to trusting Abba and believing that he can accomplish what concerns me. I can say that trusting Abba is worth it. When I recognize his goodness throughout my day, I am encouraged and able to keep focused. When things don't go as planned, I choose to believe Abba is near and ordering my steps. I believe that he is good. Then I can trust him again.

Abba will lead you well, and you can trust him to be your Lord!

We Need Other Believers in Our Life

In Psalm 16:3, we read, "As for the saints who are in the earth, they are the majestic ones in whom is all my delight." Saints are believers in Jesus. We need other believers around us who are also walking with Abba Father so we can be encouraged to keep going.

I have struggled with wanting people in my life since I felt I needed to protect myself from people. But Abba lovingly taught me that he would protect me: "The LORD is for me; I will not fear; What can man do to me?" (Psalm 118:6). Abba is for me. Wow! Abba is for you too. We can choose to say no to fear because people cannot change our destiny. People can be hard and hurtful, but the truth here is that when we trust in Abba, we don't need to fear people having power over us. No matter what happens during our day, we can stop and get Abba's perspective. He may show us how to respond, or he might just give us peace so we can rest.

For me, I had people I needed to forgive before I could begin to let others in my life. Abba began to stretch me and teach me more about forgiveness. I remember not understanding how to forgive and feeling very frustrated. One evening, I stopped and yelled at Abba, "I don't understand! How do I forgive, and how can you make things right?" Instantly I saw a vision playing out in front of me: it was of my children, and they were arguing over a glass of water. One child was complaining that their sibling had drunk their water. I thought, *I can refill your cup. It's not a problem.* Then the vision ended.

In that moment, I fully understood the vision and started laughing. I realized that I had been behaving like my children. It was as if I had been protesting to Abba, "They drank my water!" From my perspective, my loss felt too big to be fixed. But Abba was showing me how fast and easily he could restore what others had taken from me. From Abba's perspective, I was his child, and he was saying that he could restore anything—as easily as refilling a cup of water. I was blown away.

Abba Father wants us whole and set free from unforgiveness. Let's jump and decide to forgive others as Abba has forgiven us. Let's decide to trust Abba to heal our hearts and restore what was lost. I have learned to notice when I feel offended and to be quick to bring them to Abba. I choose to forgive the person in that moment and to leave the person in Abba Father's hands to deal with. I want my heart clear before Abba and not filled with bitterness or unforgiveness. This enables me to engage with other believers in a healthy way.

In the same way, Abba will show you how to engage with other believers in a wise way and how to have healthy boundaries.

We Need Abba Father to Show Us Our Hearts

Psalm 16:4 tells us, "The sorrows of those who have bartered for another god will be multiplied; I shall not pour out their drink offerings of blood, nor will I take their names upon my lips." I like to think my motives are always right and that my heart is staying in faith. Abba knows my heart and truly wants me to be free, so he gently speaks to me when I am trusting in another god besides him. Abba Father will do the same for you. Trusting in another god is simply finding solutions for yourself and not trusting in Abba for the solution. The phrase "bartering for another god" is an old-fashioned way of saying that we are finding something besides Abba to help us. The consequence of this is multiplied sorrows. Abba Father has solutions for us. We want to pause and ask Abba what his solution is so we can know our next step.

As the Israelites wandered in the desert, they had real needs for food, water, and protection, so Abba made sure they had these things. The problem was in the Israelites' hearts. They grumbled against Abba whenever they had a need (see Exodus 16:2, 8) instead of humbly asking him and trusting him to provide what they needed.

If we try to solve our problems without Abba or grumble about what we don't have, we will multiply our sorrows. This can happen in many ways, and you can ask Abba to show you if you are trusting in something besides him. Over the years, I have learned that I often try to make certain outcomes happen. But when I let go of control and wait for Abba to move, I have peace and see a better outcome.

You can trust Abba to have your best interest at heart and to have the perfect plan. Waiting for Abba is hard but worth it. Believing that Abba Father is on your side is essential for you to be able to wait for Abba to provide for you. You can trust him. He will be faithful to show you your heart and then the way to go.

OUR POSITION AS ABBA'S CHILDREN

The LORD is the portion of my inheritance
and my cup;
You support my lot.
The lines have fallen to me in pleasant places;
Indeed, my heritage is beautiful to me. (Psalm
16:5–6)

Our position is that of Abba Father's children. Because we are his children, he has provided for us an inheritance and a heritage. In my time of learning these verses, I declared these verses over myself. I chose to believe what Abba said in his Word even if it felt foreign to me. I told myself that Abba was my portion and my inheritance. My relationship with Abba was and is so valuable to me. His inheritance includes his presence, his love, his help, his healing, and his provision.

One day, I was complaining to Abba that no one was supporting me. Abba said, "I am supporting you." Instantly, Psalm 16:5 jumped into my mind—"The LORD is the portion of my inheritance and my cup; You support my lot"—and I was faced with deciding if I was going to believe Abba or continue with my own negative thoughts. I knew it was better to trust Abba's correction because he was for me. So I erased my complaining thoughts and replaced them with Abba's truth from his Word: "You support my lot." When we replace our thoughts with Abba's thoughts, our faces are lifted. We see Abba again and can interact with his love toward us.

Psalm 16:6 says Abba plans pleasant places for us and a beautiful heritage. These two thoughts of pleasant places and a beautiful heritage can be hard to see when we look around us. In order to see our beautiful heritage, we must stop looking at our earthly circumstances and look instead at Abba and what he has promised. It takes daily practice to retrain how we think and what we focus on. For me, I needed to memorize these psalms and to read them daily to retrain my way of thinking. I decided to believe that Abba had pleasant places for me in the middle of what I was walking through. I found that when I chose to agree with Abba, my thinking changed to his way of thinking. I began to see his pleasant places for me.

It is so fun and amazing to look back at my life and see the goodness of Abba. In addition to memorizing psalms, I have also found it helpful to write down the dates and details of significant events in my life—both the bad times and the good times. Then, I add the events to a timeline. I've been amazed to see that my bad times and my good times are usually in the same season of life!

One of my bad times was when I was eight years old, when my family moved away from my childhood home to San Jose, California. We lived there only three years, but those three years were awful for me. I have always hated those years and wondered why we even moved there in the first place. They felt like wasted years full of sadness.

Contrast this with one of my good times. When I was nine years old, I was invited to a Bible study for children during school lunch. It was there that I heard about Jesus and accepted him as my Lord and Savior.

Until I created my timeline, I'd never connected that both my worst time and my best time were in the same season of my life. I realized that Abba Father moved me to San Jose so I could meet him. This changed my perspective and made me happy that we moved to San Jose. It reframed the hard season of my life as I realized that Abba had been with me, guiding me the whole time. Knowing this about Abba made me love him even more. If I had not stopped and considered the good and bad events of my life, I would not have seen the goodness of Abba Father in my life.

It is hard to see beyond what is right in front of you unless you stop and interact with Abba. He will minister to your heart and lift your face. It is especially fun to see his goodness as you look back on your life. He has been and still is present in your life. He will never leave you. Look for Abba's touch in your life.

We have been given everything we need for life and godliness (see 2 Peter 1:3). Abba Father has given us himself, and he is our cup of life, as it says in Psalm 16:5. Nothing is too hard for him, and nothing is withheld from us. Abba Father supports us all along the way. Look up and see him beside you. Abba Father will direct you and lead you to pleasant places. When you rely on him, he will make your life beautiful. You can trust in him.

ABBA FATHER'S PROVISION

I will bless the LORD who has counseled me;
Indeed, my mind instructs me in the night.
I have set the LORD continually before me;
Because He is at my right hand, I will not be shaken.
Therefore my heart is glad and my glory rejoices;
My flesh also will dwell securely.
For You will not abandon my soul to Sheol;
Nor will You allow Your Holy One to undergo decay.
You will make known to me the path of life;
In Your presence is fullness of joy;
In Your right hand there are pleasures forever.
(Psalm 16:7–11)

In these verses, I see the goodness of Abba Father and his provision for me. I see that he has provided blessings and provision for my mind, heart, body, and soul. I see he has also provided his presence, which guides me. When I was first working to understand these verses, I read them day after day until I began to believe them. I rehearsed these verses to myself daily so I would remember them. These verses offer beautiful truths about the mind, heart, body, soul, and his presence, which changed the way I interacted with Abba.

Our Minds

Psalm 16:7 says, "I will bless the LORD who has counseled me; indeed, my mind instructs me in the night." This verse is a great reminder to choose to bless Abba. We bless him when we thank him or praise him. We bless Abba when we believe in his promises and trust in him. I am so grateful that Abba gently nudges my thoughts in the correct direction. He nudges my natural reaction away from the negative that I see and toward his perspective, which includes his promise.

I have found that listening to worship music helps renew my mind so that I can think and speak Abba Father's promises aloud. I find that whatever I fill my mind with in the evening influences what I wake up hearing. Abba really does instruct me in the night, and I wake up with a praise song coming from my mind. When we trust in Abba Father and in what Scripture says, we allow peace to flood our minds. Then, we are better able to recognize the promptings of Abba away from fear and toward peace.

Our Hearts

Verse eight tells us, "I have set the LORD continually before me; because He is at my right hand, I will not be shaken." This verse helped me focus my heart on Abba and his promises to me instead of focusing on my circumstances. I continually set the Lord before me by rehearsing Abba's promises to me. This rehearsing is an important part of keeping my heart focused. I let the truth that Abba is right beside me sink deep into my heart. Knowing that he is right beside me gives me peace. The phrase "I will not be shaken" has become a kind of mantra for me. It means I will believe in Abba's promises, even when I detect a problem or delay.

Declaring this verse over yourself will cleanse your heart of worldly mindsets and strengthen you. You will be better able to rely on Abba. What you say comes from your heart (see Luke 6:45) and will change your reality. I want my thoughts and my spoken words to agree with Abba and his Word. I don't want to accidentally agree with the Enemy by thinking or speaking the opposite of Abba's Word. I want to love the Lord with all my heart and be cleansed from worldly mindsets. I meditate on what Abba is seeing and saying. I want my heart to fully trust in Abba by believing him and his Word. This is what makes it possible for us to not be shaken when life is hard. Abba is faithful to hold us and to keep us.

Our Bodies

Psalm 16:9 says, "Therefore my heart is glad and my glory rejoices; my flesh also will dwell securely." This verse comes right after the previous declaration that Abba is at my right hand so I won't be shaken. Because of my certainty in Abba's nearness and in his provision for me, my heart can be glad and rejoice.

This is an important heart orientation because it affects the health of our bodies. Proverbs says, "A happy heart is good medicine and a joyful mind causes healing" (Proverbs 17:22). A glad heart that is trusting in Abba will bring healing to the body. We can decide that Abba is worthy of our trust and then rely on his care for our bodies.

This might be scary at first! As I was learning this, I made a conscious choice to believe that Abba could protect me from sickness and injury. I was secure and decided not to worry about sickness. If sickness did come, I still did not worry. Instead, I prayed and asked Abba for healing and then expected myself to become well because Abba had said my flesh would dwell securely. Sometimes, it seems that sickness is normal because of our world full of germs and illness. But we also know Abba has paid for our healing through the blood of Jesus: "By His scourging we are healed" (Isaiah 53:5). Once Jesus rose from the dead, he fulfilled Isaiah 53:5, and we can now rebuke sickness's permission to come each time we run into germs or illness. We can stop worrying and walk in peace. If sickness does come, Abba will make clear how he wants us to pray and what decisions to make. He may direct us to use medicine or to see a doctor, or he may instruct us to wait for him to heal us. Ultimately, we do not need to fear. He is always right with us. Our bodies can dwell securely.

Our Souls

Psalm 16:10 promises, "For You will not abandon my soul to Sheol; nor will You allow Your Holy One to undergo decay." The idea that Abba would not abandon my soul was key for me. I recited this to myself continually as Abba Father was healing my soul with his love and I was learning to walk with him. I made time to spend with Abba and to hear what he wanted to highlight to me in Scripture. Being with Abba was healing to my soul.

I have learned to invite Abba to minister to my soul when I have a bad memory. Instead of pushing down the bad memory, I invite him to heal my heart deep within and to give me his perspective. His perspective is filled with love and peace, power and clear thinking (see 2 Timothy 1:7). When I am in the middle of a hard situation, I have learned to pause and invite Abba to minister to me. Each time, I am refreshed, renewed, and able to continue. He can also minister to my soul when I am happy. Spending time with Abba when something good has happened is especially good for my soul. I am so grateful Abba is present and active in my life and that he cares for me. He will care for you, too! We can count on the fact that he will not abandon our souls. He cares about us and will provide what our souls need.

His Presence

The last verse of Psalm 16 says, "You will make known to me the path of life; in Your presence is fullness of joy; in Your right hand there are pleasures forever." Abba will show us the path that leads to life and the choices to make. This is incredible! He will make known to us the path of life—the path that brings us life. We will not miss it because Abba is right there with us. Let me say that again: *We will not miss the correct path to take because Abba is right there with us.*

It is good to orient our hearts to believe in this promise that Abba will make known to us the path of life. As I journey, if I feel uncertain, the temptation is for me to feel alone. At these times, I must remind myself that Abba promised to show me the path of life and that he will keep his promises. I can stop and spend time in his presence. I can ask Abba questions and expect him to answer me. Sometimes he speaks to my heart, sometimes he speaks to me through Scripture, and sometimes he speaks to me through impressions. When Abba speaks to you, it will always sound loving. As you spend time with Abba, he will give you his perspective, and you will be filled with joy that comes from him. Abba Father is so wonderful. He gives you his presence and his joy, and he has more good planned for you than you expect. His joy strengthens you, and his presence gives you security. Your job is to keep your eyes on Abba Father and his promises to you. Again, Abba Father loves you and is for you!

Abba cares about you—mind, heart, body, and soul. He asks us to love him with our whole mind, heart, body, and soul, and he heals and strengthens us in all these areas. When we trust in Abba, we can rest from trying to do life on our own. Abba is there with us, and, no matter what happens in life, we can know that he is for us.

As we close this chapter, remember:

- Your mind can rest securely knowing that Abba Father is leading you and showing you the path that leads to life.
- Your heart can rest securely knowing that Abba Father will not let you fail. He is right there with you.
- Your body can rest securely knowing that Abba Father is with you.
- Your soul can rest securely knowing that Abba Father will not abandon you.
- Abba Father's presence with you allows you to rest in his total care for you.

Abba Father is for you.

ACTIVATION

In this activation, keep in mind our two goals: (1) to connect with Abba Father and his love for you and (2) to hear Abba Father speak to you either in thought or Scripture or a picture in your mind.

Our next chapter will focus on Psalm 17 and Abba Father's protection of us in the battle. We are all in a battle of some kind. The following Recharge section will include reading Psalm 17. As you spend time with Abba reading Psalm 17, you will make space for Abba to speak to your heart about the psalm before we cover it in Chapter 3. Abba will tell you the things he wants you to know. He will speak to you and encourage your heart. You can spend as many days as you want recharging with Abba and reading Psalm 17. I recommend spending at least four days recharging before moving on. We will also reread Psalm 126 since this is our anchor promise. Abba is so good.

RECHARGE WITH ABBA FATHER

Total time: 10–15 minutes

Minutes 1–3: Silence and Reflection

Spend a few minutes sitting with Abba. To begin, recite the phrase from Psalm 46:10, "Be still and know that I am God." Shorten the phrase each time to set your heart. Notice the nuances of shortening the phrase:

> *Be still and know that I am God.*
> *Be still and know that I am.*
> *Be still and know.*
> *Be still.*
> *Be.*

For the remainder of the three minutes, sit in silence with Abba Father and just be with him. At the end, write down anything you have seen, sensed, or heard spoken to you. Remember that it is okay and normal if you do not see or sense or hear anything. Abba enjoys simply being with you.

Minutes 3–5: Reading

Read Psalm 126; then read Psalm 17.

Minutes 5–8: Journaling

Write down any verses from these psalms Abba Father has highlighted and their meaning to you. This will allow you to remember what Abba has spoken to your heart.

Minutes 8–10: Sitting with Abba

End your time by spending two minutes in silence with Abba Father. At the end, write down anything you have seen, sensed, or heard spoken to you.

Throughout your day:

Worship songs: "Prophesy Your Promise" by Mack Brock, "One Like Us" by Mack Brock, "After Me" by Mack Brock, "Do It Again" by Mack Brock

Chapter 3

The Battle

Psalm 17

¹ Hear a just cause, O LORD, give heed to my cry;
Give ear to my prayer, which is not from deceitful lips.
² Let my judgment come forth from Your presence;
Let Your eyes look with equity.
³ You have tried my heart;
You have visited me by night;
You have tested me and You find nothing;
I have purposed that my mouth will not transgress.

⁴ As for the deeds of men, by the word of Your lips
I have kept from the paths of the violent.
⁵ My steps have held fast to Your paths.
My feet have not slipped.
⁶ I have called upon You, for You will answer me, O God;
Incline Your ear to me, hear my speech.
⁷ Wondrously show Your lovingkindness,
O Savior of those who take refuge at Your right hand
From those who rise up against them.
⁸ Keep me as the apple of Your eye;
Hide me in the shadow of Your wings
⁹ From the wicked who despoil me,
My deadly enemies who surround me.
¹⁰ They have closed their unfeeling heart,
With their mouth they speak proudly.
¹¹ They have now surrounded us in our steps;
They set their eyes to cast us down to the ground.
¹² He is like a lion that is eager to tear,
And as a young lion lurking in hiding places.
¹³ Arise, O LORD, confront him, bring him low;
Deliver my soul from the wicked with Your sword,
¹⁴ From men with Your hand, O LORD,
From men of the world, whose portion is in this life,
And whose belly You fill with Your treasure;
They are satisfied with children,

And leave their abundance to their babes.
[15] As for me, I shall behold Your face in righteousness;
I will be satisfied with Your likeness when I awake.

We have seen that Abba Father is good and that he is for us. These are the first steps in being able to trust Abba. Now, we will get to see Abba Father as our protector. We are not alone; Abba is with us. In Psalm 17, we will explore our proper attitude toward Abba Father, Abba Father's strength, the Enemy's tactics, and our resulting shift in perspective once we know the truth.

You are not alone, and you can count on Abba to be with you and to be your protector.

OUR ATTITUDE TOWARD ABBA FATHER

Hear a just cause, O LORD, give heed to my cry;
Give ear to my prayer, which is not from deceitful lips.
Let my judgment come forth from Your presence;
Let Your eyes look with equity.
You have tried my heart;
You have visited me by night;
You have tested me and You find nothing;
I have purposed that my mouth will not transgress.

As for the deeds of men, by the word of Your
lips
I have kept from the paths of the violent.
My steps have held fast to Your paths.
My feet have not slipped. (Psalm 17:1–5)

These first five verses in Psalm 17 have challenged me to orient my heart humbly before Abba Father. It has been a journey of learning how to trust him and letting him guide me, and as I look back, I can say this journey was worth it. The prize in this journey is the privilege of getting to know Abba and walking with him.

At the beginning of this journey, I focused on ways I had been wronged. I wanted Abba to make things right. This mode made me position myself against people and what they did. I began to realize that I was in a battle for my heart. Was I going to fight my own battle and demand justice from God? Or was I going to set aside my rights in favor of a relationship with a loving Abba Father and let him fight my battle? I wanted the relationship with Abba! I knew that having a humble, teachable heart would change my focus and the way I heard Scripture. I memorized these verses and then positioned myself to believe that Abba loved me and was working on my behalf. This set me up to grow. Even though I could still see weaknesses in myself, I began to see myself the way Abba described me in these five verses. This began to change my heart. I found that when I felt loved, I didn't need to position myself against people. I could simply love them instead.

I see two main areas for heart change in these verses—wanting Abba's perspective and wanting Abba's refining. Let's look at both of these areas.

Wanting Abba's Perspective

Psalm 17:1 starts right out validating that our perspective is correct and not deceitful: "Hear a just cause, O LORD, give heed to my cry; give ear to my prayer, which is not from deceitful lips." I can identify with that. I am able to honestly assess the situation, to see right from wrong, and to identify the wrong thing that has happened. Justice seems simple to me. But as I allow myself to sit with Abba, I begin to see that my perspective is not the whole picture—Abba's is. I love that verse two switches to acknowledging that Abba Father's perspective is the only correct perspective: "Let my judgment come forth from Your presence; let Your eyes look with equity." Abba is gentle and loving, and all his judgments are kind and loving. His judgments are far better than we could dream. We can trust him. I want to hear *his* judgment, which will be full of grace and mercy, not the judgment of people. I want *his* equity in my life, not my version of equity. Abba Father's way is far better than my way.

One day, I was in a meeting and felt I was being unfairly judged by my failures. I wanted them to think well of me and felt angry at the conversation about me. I could tell that Abba Father was highlighting my feelings of anger and wanted to talk to me about them. Later I sat with Abba and asked him why I was so mad. What did he want to tell me? He revealed that I had been looking for my approval from people, but he wanted me to get my approval from him. I repented of my misplaced devotion, and my anger flowed away. I was released from the desire to impress people or to be approved of by people.

When I get my approval and judgment from Abba, I am better able to let go of injustices. I can trust that Abba will have things turn out for my good. It has been very freeing for me to trust that Abba has my best interest at heart. It is freeing to believe that his viewpoint is the best for me. I can let go of control easier when I am trusting Abba and his perspective.

Wanting Abba's Refining

Psalm 17:3–5 identifies the process Abba Father uses to test our hearts, shows us what our hearts are capable of, and declares that he is able to hold us and keep our feet from slipping: "You have tried my heart; You have visited me by night; You have tested me, and You find nothing; I have purposed that my mouth will not transgress. As for the deeds of men, by the word of Your lips I have kept from the paths of the violent. My steps have held fast to Your paths. My feet have not slipped."

Abba Father cares for us. He cares about our hearts and tests us to help us grow. We can position our hearts correctly by declaring the end of verse three: "I have purposed that my mouth will not transgress." This is our invitation for Abba Father to refine us and search our heart.

Psalm 139:23–24 tells us, "Search me, O God, and know my heart; try me and know my anxious thoughts; and see if there be any hurtful way in me and lead me in the everlasting way."

Now, in the past I have been afraid of these two verses from Psalm 139 because it sounded like all my "stuff" would be exposed. I preferred hiding to being exposed. But I realized that Abba was not trying to expose me. He loved me and wanted to set me free. Also, I wasn't actually able to hide from Abba. He was waiting for me to invite him to search my heart. I started seeing these two verses as proof that Abba saw and cared about me. He knew I had anxious thoughts and wanted to help me stay in peace and trust. Abba didn't want me to hurt myself; he wanted to lead me in the everlasting way—the way of life.

He is aware of your anxiety, too. He wants to protect you from the things inside you that hurt you. When you yield to Abba and let him shape you, you will follow in the way of life and avoid many pitfalls.

As I learned how to trust in Abba's care for me, I was able to orient my heart to desire his refining. I wanted to break free from my familiar ways of thinking that didn't line up with Abba's way of thinking. We all have ways of reacting inside of us that are not the way Abba would act.

Memorizing Scripture has really helped me to orient my thoughts toward Abba in all sorts of circumstances. One day, I was offended by my husband and thinking about how to get back at him. I was really mad! But then Abba highlighted Psalm 17:4 to me, which warns about responding to people in wrong ways: "As for the deeds of men, by the word of Your lips I have kept from the paths of the violent." I wanted to believe my thoughts were right, but they certainly were not in that moment. Abba showed me I was heading my own way down a path that would make things worse. I repented of trying to make things right on my own and moved back into a place of trust in Abba. That enabled me to forgive the offense and trust Abba to handle it for me.

This moment grappling with my anger was the first time I really understood what it meant to be "kept from the paths of the violent." It was an aha moment where I realized how easy it was to get off of Abba's path and how much I needed Abba's Word to keep my feet from slipping. Psalm 17:5 says, "My steps have held fast to Your paths. My feet have not slipped." If I want my feet to not slip and to hold to his paths, I must keep away from my old ways of thinking and check my thoughts against Scripture. Memorizing and meditating on Scripture has given Abba space to speak to my heart when direction or correction is needed. He is pleased with me when I learn from my mistakes.

Please keep in mind that it is not your perfection that keeps you from slipping. Walking with Abba Father and responding to him is what keeps you from slipping.

When I memorize Scripture and listen to music that agrees with Scripture, my mind is constantly thinking about Scripture. I wake up hearing a song in my mind, and throughout the day, I'm reminded by Abba of different passages. This is part of retraining my mind to think the way Abba thinks. Soaking in God's Word keeps our steps on the right paths and is one way he protects us. We must be intentional to read Scripture again and again and let Abba Father reveal things about it so that it sinks deep into us. Then we will hold fast to the path of Abba, our protector.

ABBA FATHER'S STRENGTH

I have called upon You, for You will answer
me, O God;
Incline Your ear to me, hear my speech.
Wondrously show Your lovingkindness,
O Savior of those who take refuge at Your
right hand
From those who rise up against them.
Keep me as the apple of Your eye;
Hide me in the shadow of Your wings
From the wicked who despoil me,
My deadly enemies who surround me. (Psalm
17:6–9)

Abba Father is strong, and nothing is hard for him. He welcomes us to stand behind him as he deals with our bullies. I love that these verses start out by declaring that Abba will listen to us and answer us.

Abba Father is already oriented toward you to listen to you and to show you his loving-kindness. Abba loves you so much and has set you as the apple of his eye—his favorite one. You are so valuable to Abba. He invites you to take refuge at his right hand when others are against you. It's a neat picture: you need rest, and Abba hides you in himself so you can rest. He is so strong and able to deal with our deadly enemies who surround us, as verse nine says.

The wicked and the deadly enemies are not people—this is important to know. The wicked and the deadly enemies are the unseen powers in the spiritual realm: "For our struggle is not against flesh and blood, but against the rulers, against the powers, against the world forces of this darkness, against the spiritual forces of wickedness in the heavenly places" (Ephesians 6:12). This might sound like a very big list of powerful demons and spiritual forces of wickedness. But we must remember there is no one like Abba Father and not one of these spiritual forces of wickedness can stand against Abba. Abba Father is the living God. All of the spiritual forces of wickedness are already conquered because of the death and resurrection of Jesus. We are safe with Abba Father. All we need to do is recognize our need and cry out to Abba.

Abba will listen to us and answer us, and he will show us his loving-kindness. Abba is right there beside us; we can take refuge at Abba's right hand. You can run to him, and he will keep you safe. Abba provides rest and restoration for us while he is dealing with the Enemy. We can trust this; we can trust Abba.

Psalm 16:10 says, "You will not abandon my soul." I believe Abba will not abandon my soul. I believe Abba will restore my soul and provide for me. I run to Abba daily or more often than daily to refresh my soul. I don't want to struggle with my own limited perspective; I need Abba's perspective on a situation, and I need to hear Abba's declaration about who I am.

Psalm 17:2 says, "Let my judgment come forth from your presence." I am his beloved daughter. That is his judgment about me. That is his judgment about you too. You are Abba's beloved child. Abba will keep you safe and hide you so you can rest. He will guide you with his loving-kindness and show you the path of life. Abba Father is your protector.

THE ENEMY'S TACTICS

They have closed their unfeeling heart,
With their mouth they speak proudly.
They have now surrounded us in our steps;
They set their eyes to cast us down to the
ground.
He is like a lion that is eager to tear,
And as a young lion lurking in hiding places.
(Psalm 17:10–12)

These verses sound intimidating, but the proper perspective is that the Enemy is no match for Abba Father. No match! There is no comparison at all. All the Enemy can do is speak lies to us and attempt to overwhelm us. The Enemy will try to make us feel alone and vulnerable by making us feel surrounded. Notice that the Enemy does not have any real power over us. He can only lie, speak proudly, put us down, make us feel alone, scare us, and worry us. He cannot touch us! When we fully embrace that we are not alone and Abba is with us, we are liberated and our hearts are drawn in love toward Abba.

One cry from us, and Abba Father gives us the correct perspective. We must check *all* the thoughts that come against us to see if the thought matches what Abba says. We often don't realize that our negative thoughts are from the Enemy. Lies like "I can't do that" or "God is unhappy with me" or

"I'm unqualified" are not from Abba Father! So first, we must learn to recognize these as negative thoughts. Second, we must recognize that Abba will not say negative things to us. Therefore, these thoughts are lies from the Enemy. Third, we want to think Abba's truths and get Abba's point of view. Seeing from Abba's point of view will quickly silence the Enemy. Finally, we must speak out Abba's truths until they are our own thoughts as well.

Abba is saying to you, "You can do this." He says, "I am so happy with you." He assures you, "I am the one who qualifies you and calls you." When you begin to believe Abba's truths, it doesn't matter where the Enemy "hides" because you are quick to recognize the Enemy's lies and speak Abba's truth. Let's settle this: Abba Father is stronger than the Enemy and will protect you. Abba Father is your protector.

OUR SHIFT IN PERSPECTIVE

> Arise, O LORD, confront him, bring him low;
> Deliver my soul from the wicked with Your sword,
> From men with Your hand, O LORD,
> From men of the world, whose portion is in this life,
> And whose belly You fill with Your treasure;
> They are satisfied with children,
> And leave their abundance to their babes.
> As for me, I shall behold Your face in righteousness;
> I will be satisfied with Your likeness when I awake. (Psalm 17:13–15)

Our old perspective is that the Enemy seems strong, we seem weak, and God seems far away. Our shift to a proper perspective is that the Enemy is weak, we are strong, and Abba Father is near us and already acting on our behalf. This is wonderful! We can call on Abba to defeat the Enemy and minister to our souls. This part of Psalm 17 proves we can call on Abba to keep us from the worldly mindset of those around us. These verses are not merely confronting fixations on money or children. They are asking the question, "What is our portion?" The middle of this section shows a mindset of someone who thinks their portion is limited to satisfaction in this life. But God wants more for us: he wants us to "behold [his] face in righteousness." Our portion is our relationship with Abba, and we are satisfied only with the Lord.

Psalm 16:6 says, "My heritage is beautiful to me." Abba has a beautiful heritage planned for us. He plans to prosper us and to bless us, which includes relationship with him—as well as money and children. It comes down to our focus. Are we setting Abba Father in front of us and trusting in him? We want Abba to protect us from a worldly focus that makes worry comfortable to us. The right focus is to trust in Abba and have a close connection with Abba Father. He loves you so much and is near to you.

Abba Father is your protector.

ACTIVATION

Abba Father loves you with an unending love. There is nothing you can do to make Abba change his mind about you. He treasures you and thinks about you with loving thoughts. Keep this in mind as you progress through this activation.

Chapter 4 will focus on Psalm 37:1–11 and Abba Father's plan. When we follow Abba's plans, there is rest. The following Recharge section will include reading Psalm 37:1-11, and I encourage you to spend time with Abba reading this psalm before reading the next chapter in this book. Make room for Abba to highlight things to you. You will be encouraged. You can spend as many days as you want recharging with Abba and reading Psalm 37:1–11. I recommend spending at least four days recharging before moving on. Again, we will also read Psalm 126 since this is our anchor promise. Abba is so good.

RECHARGE WITH ABBA FATHER

Total time: 10–15 minutes

Minutes 1–3: Silence and Reflection

Spend a few minutes sitting with Abba. To begin, recite the phrase from Psalm 46:10, "Be still and know that I am God." Shorten the phrase each time to set your heart. Notice the nuances of shortening the phrase:

Be still and know that I am God.
Be still and know that I am.
Be still and know.
Be still.
Be.

For the remainder of the three minutes, sit in silence with Abba Father and just be with him. At the end, write down anything you have seen, sensed, or heard spoken to you. Do not worry if you do not see or sense or hear anything. Abba enjoys simply being with you.

Minutes 3–5: Reading

Read Psalm 126; then read Psalm 37:1–11.

Minutes 5–8: Journaling

Write down any verses from these psalms Abba Father has highlighted and their meaning to you. This will allow you to remember what Abba has spoken to your heart.

Minutes 8–10: Sitting with Abba

End your time by spending two minutes in silence with Abba Father. At the end, write down anything you have seen, sensed, or heard spoken to you.

Throughout your day:

Worship songs: "You Reign" by Mack Brock, "Even the Impossible" by Mack Brock, "Still I Will Praise" by Mack Brock, "To the End" by Mack Brock

Chapter 4

The Plan

Psalm 37:1–11

[1] Do not fret because of evildoers,
Be not envious toward wrongdoers.
[2] For they will wither quickly like the grass
And fade like the green herb.
[3] Trust in the LORD and do good;
Dwell in the land and cultivate faithfulness.
[4] Delight yourself in the LORD;
And He will give you the desires of your heart.
[5] Commit your way to the LORD,
Trust also in Him, and He will do it.
[6] He will bring forth your righteousness as the light
And your judgment as the noonday.

[7] Rest in the LORD and wait patiently for Him;
Do not fret because of him who prospers in his way,
Because of the man who carries out wicked schemes.
[8] Cease from anger and forsake wrath;
Do not fret; it leads only to evildoing.
[9] For evildoers will be cut off,
But those who wait for the LORD, they will inherit the land.
[10] Yet a little while and the wicked man will be no more;
And you will look carefully for his place and he will not be there.
[11] But the humble will inherit the land
And will delight themselves in abundant prosperity.

Abba Father loves us and has a plan for us. The incredible thing is that he sees each one of us and knows us individually. In Psalm 37, Abba lovingly lets us know how to walk so we can be successful and avoid disaster. The plan starts with trusting in Abba and resting in him in security. It results in us inheriting more than we hoped for, which we see echoed throughout Scripture: "O taste and see that the Lord is good; how blessed is the man who takes refuge in Him!" (Psalm 34:8).

TRUST IN ABBA FATHER

Do not fret because of evildoers,
Be not envious toward wrongdoers.
For they will wither quickly like the grass
And fade like the green herb.
Trust in the LORD and do good;
Dwell in the land and cultivate faithfulness.
Delight yourself in the LORD;
And He will give you the desires of your
heart. (Psalm 37:1–4)

Psalm 37 starts off with Abba Father instructing us not to fret about evildoers or wrongdoers. *Fret* is a word we do not use much anymore. The definition of *fret* is "to be constantly or visibly worried or anxious."[1] Fretting is a state of mind where we feel responsible for making sure things are fair for us. If you live your life worried about being wronged, you will struggle to believe there is something good for you besides what you see in front of you. Abba Father has something good for you. Abba draws our attention to himself. We have the chance to set our mind and our heart to trust in Abba and to believe in his promise to us. What you see—your circumstance—is not the whole story. Abba Father sees you and has good plans for you. Abba instructs you to not fret or to desire the results that come from making plans on your own.

I am getting better at letting go of control, letting go of my plan, and letting Abba direct me. I once had an experience with Abba that showed me his ability to handle what concerned

---

1   "fret" (Google search for "definition of fret"), *The Oxford English Dictionary*, OED Labs, accessed December 4, 2024.

me: I could sense my family was going to move but didn't know when. I was excited about moving but decided to wait for Abba's direction and not try to make it happen. It was two years before I felt Abba saying, "Yes, now." We had lived in our home for twenty-five years, and my husband liked where we lived. He was comfortable in our home. That June, we talked about moving but only briefly—I felt we would move in September. By early July, we still had not made a decision together on whether or not to move. I told Abba Father that if he wanted us to move, he would have to convince my husband and bring us a home. So, I waited some more. By the time July ended, the inkling that we would move in September was gone. I decided to rest in Abba's timing, to trust him, and not to fret.

Then, on August 1, everything changed. That morning, we were made aware of a house for sale in the town where I wanted to move. We went and looked at the house, and even my husband liked it. It was the perfect place for us. My husband talked with our banker, and we placed an offer on the house on August 3, which was accepted. We readied our own house for sale, and it sold immediately with a closing date of September 30. Our first night in our new house was September 30. I was blown away that Abba had been able to accomplish everything we needed and had moved us in September after all. It was a whirlwind, but it was also so wonderful to see how Abba could do things.

Trusting in Abba is essential if we are to wait for his timing. Verse two says, "For they will wither quickly like the grass and fade like the green herb." The people who are not trusting Abba to lead them will burn out quickly. They will not be able to persevere. It is our destiny and our legacy that are on the line. Will we follow Abba's timetable and trust in him? Will we capture our thoughts and realign them with Abba's?

Psalm 37:3–4 gives us Abba's plan for us. We are told first to trust in Abba and to follow his lead by doing good to others. Trusting in Abba is possible when we realize Abba sees us and is with us. He is worthy of our trust, and he can be trusted to accomplish what he has promised. Second, we are told to be present where we are and to be faithful in the small things. The opposite of being present where we are is longing for what is behind us or ahead of us. Both ways of interacting with our circumstances, whether looking to the past or the future, will bring us stress. When we are present in our circumstances, we will be able to process what is happening. Abba is interested in how we are processing our circumstances. He wants to give us peace. When we trust in him and are faithful in the small things, we will have his peace and not need to worry.

Peace is valuable to us. Having peace lets us delight in our relationship with Abba. When we delight ourselves in Abba, he will help us discover and reawaken the dreams and desires deep in our hearts. He loves partnering with us. You can trust your life to Abba because he cares about you (see 1 Peter 5:7). Abba Father sees you.

REST AND SECURITY

Commit your way to the LORD,
Trust also in Him, and He will do it.
He will bring forth your righteousness as the
light
And your judgment as the noonday.
Rest in the LORD and wait patiently for Him;
Do not fret because of him who prospers in
his way,
Because of the man who carries out wicked
schemes. (Psalm 37:5–7)

Abba is amazing. He invites us to commit our way to him and trust in him; and he says that he will accomplish what we are committing to him. I find Psalm 37:5 very freeing. Abba is revealing that we can trust in him and feel secure. Abba will direct your life in the right way every time, but his way of working in your life will be much more than a fix for your circumstances. Verse six says he will go beyond this and work righteousness in you.

I am always surprised that Abba has a bigger picture in mind. His ways always turn out better than I could have imagined. He loves me and is the one who died for me, so I can trust that he will be working in my favor. I don't know the timing, but I do know that Abba is faithful. He will do it. This means you do not need to fear! Abba will be working in your favor because He loves you. Abba Father invites us into a relationship with him where we patiently walk with him, waiting for his good timing to be complete.

Verse seven shows us that Abba offers us rest in him while we are waiting and walking with him. We are instructed not to fret and worry—just rest while we wait. The word *rest* means "to cease work or movement in order to relax, refresh oneself, or recover strength." It also means "to be placed or supported so as to stay in a specified position."[2]

The first definition shows us we do not need to make things happen. Abba is the one who will make things happen. As we rest, we learn there is no need to control our schedules, our circumstances, or people. We trust that Abba will get us a good outcome. As we wait for Abba's timing, we are refreshed and strengthened (see Isaiah 40:31). This is amazing and very much needed. The second meaning of rest—to be placed or supported so as to stay in a specified position—shows us that we are supported by Abba when we wait for him. Being supported is important to me. I feel peace knowing that Abba supports me (see Psalm 16:5), and I feel confident and secure knowing that Abba sees me and cares about me. Resting in the Lord allows you to stay in the mindset that Abba sees you, supports you, and will accomplish what concerns you.

THE CANOE VISION

In one of my prayer times with Abba Father, I had a vision of a canoe. This vision showed me both what life was like when I was trying to control my circumstances, and also what life was like when I am at rest in Abba. Canoes tip over easily, and the assumption is that we are supposed to do whatever

---

2   "rest" (Yahoo search for "rest"), *The Oxford English Dictionary,* Oxford Languages, accessed December 4, 2024.

it takes to stay in control so that our canoes do not tip over. But Abba said otherwise in this vision:

I'm in a canoe and the water is choppy. I have a rhythm in the canoe that keeps it from capsizing. When the other person leans too far so that the canoe threatens to tip over, I counter by leaning the other way until I am crazily hanging off the side. I am not even aware that my actions are not healthy and are the wrong way to be in a canoe. When Abba Father makes changes, I don't know what to do to maintain control. I feel on the verge of capsizing and want to jump ship or gain control by leaning into my own ideas.

Abba Father says, "No! Let me have control. Trust in me."

It is a crazy moment. What will I do? Do I rest in Abba? Do I trust him? I want healthy rhythms in my life, so I let go of control and lean on Abba. He can keep my canoe from capsizing, but if it capsizes, I know that I am positioned correctly in him (see John 15:4). Abba Father loves me (see John 16:27). Abba Father works all things for my good (see Romans 8:28). I can trust him. I don't need to hold it all together. Abba Father is my refuge and my sustenance. He gives my soul what I need. I can look to him for my direction for the day and let him lead me. I let Abba have control of the canoe.

No one can stop Abba's good plans for you. When you are walking through something difficult, this is the time to focus on Abba instead of your trouble. He is the faithful one who is always working in your life and in your favor. When you pause to be with Abba Father, you will find that he is right beside you, caring for you. You can trust in Abba to take care of what concerns you. Jesus said, "I have told you these things, so that in me you may have *peace*. In this world you will have trouble. *But take heart!* I have overcome the world" (John 16:33, NIV, emphasis mine).

When we lose our peace and begin to fret, it is a signal that we are struggling to trust Abba has our best interest in mind. In these moments, Abba can help us to trust him and to say no to fear. In Psalm 37:7, Abba reminds us to keep our eyes on him, to wait for him, and not to fret. Abba is faithful. He is keeping his eye on us. We are the apple of his eye, and he loves us. Abba will bring beauty from our pain and loss (ashes), and we will be called an oak of righteousness (see Isaiah 61:3). Abba will help us not to fret, fixate on other people, or compare our circumstances to others' circumstances. We can let go of control and lean on Abba. He will work all things for our good. We can trust him.

YOUR INHERITANCE

Cease from anger and forsake wrath;
Do not fret; it leads only to evildoing.
For evildoers will be cut off,
But those who wait for the LORD, they will inherit the land.
Yet a little while and the wicked man will be no more;
And you will look carefully for his place and he will not be there.
But the humble will inherit the land

And will delight themselves in abundant prosperity. (Psalm 37:8–11)

Abba Father is so kind to warn us of the wrong path in life and reveal our glorious inheritance that comes from following his lead. He says we must let go of anger, wrath, and fretting. It is an intentional decision not to rely on our feelings to make things right but to walk in peace with and trust in Abba. Anger, wrath, and fretting lead to evildoing and being cut off from life. *Evildoing* is not a word we use very much and is usually reserved for something very bad. The definition of evildoing, though, is much simpler: it simply refers to the violation of a law or a duty or moral principle.

If we allow anger, wrath, and fretting to guide our life, we are missing Abba's basic commandments to love him with everything we are and to love others. When we feel anger, anxiety, offense, or greed, we can know we are heading our own way and not following Abba's way. We can stop and ask Abba what his perspective is and what the truth is. He will have a different perspective and show us his truths, which will give peace to our hearts.

Psalm 37:9 says, "For evildoers will be cut off, but those who wait for the LORD, they will inherit the land." Our inheritance and our legacy are at stake when we choose to follow our own plan and let our emotions rule our decisions. Abba calls us to wait for him and his timing. Our promise in Psalm 126:6 says, "He who goes to and fro weeping, carrying his bag of seed, shall indeed come again with a shout of joy, bringing his sheaves with him." This verse has both sides of the emotional spectrum—weeping and joy. But the person in the verse is not letting his emotions dictate his path. He has kept on the path that Abba has for him, knowing that Abba promises him a great harvest filled with joy. When we humble ourselves and wait for Abba Father, we will inherit the land he has for us.

What is the land Abba Father has for you? Abba wants to partner with you to have a great harvest. He wants to do it with you.

I am encouraged by the truth that people cannot stop what Abba has planned. If I trust in Abba, I can wait on him with confidence, knowing he is walking with me. In my mind, the waiting is long, but it is during the waiting that Abba works on the rough spots in me. Psalm 37:10 says, "Yet a little while and the wicked man will be no more; and you will look carefully for his place, and he will not be there." While I am waiting and as I am humble, Abba is making things right. There will come a time where I will look carefully for the effects of the Enemy, and they will be gone. Wow! That is amazing!

When you say yes to Abba and wait for him, you will have rest, peace, and prosperity. You will be filled with delight at the abundant prosperity Abba has for you (see Psalm 37:11). Abba Father is so good and generous. He is right beside you, helping you. Our choice is simple: be angry and worry about what is not working out, or stop fretting and wait for Abba. If we stop having anger and worry in our minds, we will be able to wait for the Lord, and we will inherit the land he has for us. Abba Father is personally present with you and has good planned for you. It is satisfying to walk with Abba.

Abba Father sees you.

ACTIVATION

I hope you are finding it easier now to sit in silence with Abba and be with him. I love my focused time with Abba. If my mind wanders during my time of silence, I take notice of what I'm thinking about. If I'm worrying, I give that to Abba again and ask for his input. If I'm stuck in a bad memory, I invite him into the memory to heal my heart. Sometimes Abba gives me instructions. I try to see where my thoughts go because that will probably be his leading. Sometimes we just sit in silence. Abba Father wants to interact with you. He considers you his valuable son or daughter and will speak to your heart.

Keep this in mind as you progress through this activation. Our next chapter will focus on Psalm 40:1–5 and Abba Father's faithfulness. I encourage you to spend time with Abba in the following Recharge section reading Psalm 40:1–5 before reading Chapter 5. Make room for Abba to highlight things to you. Write down what you sense he is saying to you. You can spend as many days as you want recharging with Abba and reading Psalm 40:1–5. I recommend spending at least four days recharging before moving on. As always, we will also read Psalm 126 since this is our anchor promise. Abba is so good.

RECHARGE WITH ABBA FATHER

Total time: 10–15 minutes

Minutes 1–3: Silence and Reflection

Spend a few minutes sitting with Abba. To begin, recite the phrase from Psalm 46:10, "Be still and know that I am God." Shorten the phrase each time to set your heart. Notice the nuances of shortening the phrase:

> *Be still and know that I am God.*
> *Be still and know that I am.*
> *Be still and know.*
> *Be still.*
> *Be.*

For the remainder of the three minutes, sit in silence with Abba Father and just be with him. At the end, write down anything you have seen, sensed, or heard spoken to you.

Minutes 3–5: Reading

Read Psalm 126; then read Psalm 40:1–5.

Minutes 5–8: Journaling

Write down any verses from these psalms Abba Father has highlighted and their meaning to you. This will allow you to remember what Abba has spoken to your heart.

Minutes 8–10: Sitting with Abba

End your time by spending two minutes in silence with Abba Father. At the end, write down anything you have seen, sensed, or heard spoken to you.

Throughout your day:

Worship songs: "What a Good God" by Mack Brock, "Still in Control" by Mack Brock, "Come Now" by Mack Brock, "Just Like You've Always Done" by Mack Brock

Chapter 5

The Faithfulness

Psalm 40:1–5

¹ I waited patiently for the LORD;
And He inclined to me and heard my cry.
² He brought me up out of the pit of
destruction, out of the miry clay,
And He set my feet upon a rock making my
footsteps firm.
³ He put a new song in my mouth, a song of
praise to our God;
Many will see and fear
And will trust in the LORD.
⁴ How blessed is the man who has made the
LORD his trust,
And has not turned to the proud, nor to those
who lapse into falsehood.

⁵ Many, O Lord my God, are the wonders
which You have done,
And Your thoughts toward us;
There is none to compare with You.
If I would declare and speak of them,
They would be too numerous to count.

One of the amazing things about Abba Father is his ability to restore our life to his original design for us. Abba loves you and has not forgotten about you. Abba remembers your desires and is actively working in your life. He will bring healing to your life and restoration to your hopes and dreams. In Psalm 40:1–5, we see Abba's salvation and love, as well as his faithfulness to us. Abba Father will be faithful to you, and nothing is too hard for him. He will be faithful to restore you.

ABBA FATHER'S SALVATION

I waited patiently for the Lord;
And He inclined to me and heard my cry.
He brought me up out of the pit of destruction,
out of the miry clay,
And He set my feet upon a rock making my
footsteps firm.
He put a new song in my mouth, a song of
praise to our God;
Many will see and fear
And will trust in the Lord. (Psalm 40:1–3)

We might not always recognize what Abba is doing, but we can trust him to be active in our lives now and in the future.

I take great comfort in Psalm 40:1. It feels like Abba Father is listening to me and acknowledging that I am waiting patiently for him to answer my prayers. Sometimes we can look back and have a better view of Abba's rescue than when it was happening in the moment. Verse two says that not only does he pull us out of a pit and get us unstuck, but he also sets our feet upon a rock. We are restored to a stable foundation. Our stable foundation is acting on what we are learning from Abba (see the parable of the wise and the foolish men who built their houses on rock and on sand in Luke 6:46–49).

Abba is our restorer. Restoration means "to bring back to a former condition." There are things that happen in our lives that knock us down and seem to disqualify us, but Abba doesn't judge the way we judge. Abba says our shortcomings don't disqualify us, and rather, he *qualifies* us.

Romans 11:29 offers a stunning promise: "For the gifts and the calling of God are irrevocable." Think about that: Abba Father's gifts inside of you and his calling on your life are irrevocable. In his restoration, Abba is able to bring back your dreams and erase all disqualification, whether real or perceived. Abba Father doesn't change his mind about you. He loves you no matter what and daily saves you. Abba sets your feet firmly on the rock of his love for you and restores you. He wants to partner with you to bring about his dreams and your dreams.

Verse three says, "He put a new song in my mouth, a song of praise to our God; many will see and fear and will trust in the Lord." I certainly have found myself loving Abba and singing my own worship songs to him all the time. Abba has done a great restoration and renewing in my life, and I am full of praise to him. I thank him for pulling me out of the pit and setting my feet on a firm foundation. For me, one of the biggest "pits" was false beliefs about my worth. But I renewed my mind until I believed I was his treasured daughter. Another big pit was my dysfunctional relationship patterns. But Abba brought me books to read and people to encourage me. I learned how to walk in his peace and how to change my responses. I am forever grateful. The verse says others will trust in Abba because of my praise to him. Amazing! People will see my praise and begin to trust in Abba. What a wonderful promise.

Abba is working in your favor. You can count on his faithfulness to you. He will rescue you and save you. He will put your feet firmly on the rock and fill your mouth with a new song of praise. Keep your focus on his faithfulness, his goodness toward you, and on his promises to you. You will see Abba Father's salvation and his restoration to you day by day. Your praise to Abba will resonate with people, and many will trust in the Lord. It's an amazing promise that Abba can restore the hard parts of our story and draw others to him through our praise! Abba Father is your restorer.

ABBA FATHER'S LOVE TOWARD US

How blessed is the man who has made the
LORD his trust,
And has not turned to the proud, nor to those
who lapse into falsehood.
Many, O LORD my God, are the wonders
which You have done,

And Your thoughts toward us;
There is none to compare with You.
If I would declare and speak of them,
They would be too numerous to count.
(Psalm 40:4–5)

Abba Father is a wonderful father. You will be blessed if you trust in Abba to lead your life. It can be so easy to ignore Abba and simply turn to whatever has helped us in the past. It is familiar, and we like knowing what will most likely happen. But Psalm 40:4 is warning us not to turn to prideful people who do not acknowledge Abba in their life or whose words do not match the truths of Scripture. It is easy and convenient to let others tell us which direction to head instead of turning to Abba Father for our direction. I encourage you to remember that you are Abba's child. He will speak to you. You can hear him speak to you. Reciting these verses in Psalm 40 is a good way to train our hearts to believe in Abba and to hear him. Abba is teaching us he is trustworthy and faithful. We want to become familiar with Abba and his faithfulness.

I have learned to wait for Abba and to lean into peace and rest, even though I do not know what his timing will be. Waiting is hard, but waiting without trusting Abba is practically impossible. When I spend time in Abba Father's presence, I hear his loving thoughts toward me. I recount all his goodness to me, and I recount all his promises to me. Learning to trust Abba is what makes waiting in peace possible.

Verse five reminds us Abba has done many wonders, and there is no one like Abba Father. The verse goes on to say he loves us and thinks about us so much that we couldn't even count all his loving thoughts about us. Wow! Let the truth of verse five sink into your heart. Abba Father loves you more than you realize. You are precious to him, and his thoughts about you are for your good. Look around and see the many wonders Abba Father has done in your life. He has more good things planned for you. Abba Father has love for you and complete acceptance of you right now. He has healing and restoration for your heart. When you spend time in Abba's presence and surround yourself with these truths, you will be healed and restored. Abba Father is your restorer.

WHAT DOES FAITH LOOK LIKE?

Patiently Waiting

In the book of Hebrews, we read, "For when God made the promise to Abraham, since he could swear by no one greater, he swore by himself, saying, 'I will surely bless you and I will surely multiply you.' And so, having *patiently waited*, [Abraham] obtained the promise" (Hebrews 6:13–15, emphasis mine).

Abba Father is faithful. We see that Abraham waited patiently for Abba and obtained his promise. We might assume that the waiting was easy or quick for Abraham, but it was not easy or quick. Having a promise from Abba is fun and exciting, but waiting for the promise takes patience. Our nature is to wait a long time and then give up. Don't give up! If you surround yourself with Abba's truths, you will be able to wait for Abba's promise. Abraham continued in faith and did not give up, and he got his promise.

What anchors us to Abba? Our anchor is hope in Abba's words: "This hope we have as an anchor of the soul, a hope both sure and steadfast and one which enters within the veil" (Hebrews 6:19). Earlier, in verse sixteen, we read that an oath is something you can count on, and verse seventeen says God made an oath to keep his promise to Abraham. Verse eighteen says God cannot lie, so we can put our hope in his words. Hope is our anchor to Abba, but it is much more than an anchor. Hope is intimacy with Abba Father.

The phrase in Hebrews 6:19 that speaks of hope as something that "enters within the veil" refers to the thick curtain that separated the innermost room, the holy of holies, from the rest of the tabernacle and temple (see Exodus 26:33). This veil separated the Israelite people from God's intimate presence, and no one was allowed inside the holy of holies except the high priest once a year, when he would ask for forgiveness for the people's sins (see Hebrews 9:2–7). When Jesus died on the cross, God ripped the veil in two from top to bottom (see Mark 15:38). This signified that the barrier between us and God had been removed. We can now enter within the veil and experience God's presence, his forgiveness, and his mercy. Entering within the veil means being in an intimate place with Abba Father. Abba invites us to know him. In this intimate place, Abba will speak to us, minister to our hurt hearts, give us new hope, and guide and direct us.

Abba sets hope in front of us. We can take hold of this hope and let it anchor our souls. Waiting can be difficult when life feels like a storm and we are being tossed around by the waves. But when we do life with Abba, we have peace even in the crazy storm. Psalm 16:8 says, "I have set the Lord continually before me; because He is at my right hand, I will not be shaken." For hope to anchor us, we choose to keep our eyes on Abba and not on our circumstances. We keep our eyes on the fact that he is right beside us. We declare over and over: "I will not be shaken."

We need connection with Abba daily. Abba is present with you in all that you do throughout your day. Let him walk with you each day all the way until you obtain the promise.

Trust in Abba's Word

Hebrews 11:1–2 says, "Now faith is the assurance of things hoped for, the conviction of things not seen. For by it the men of old gained approval." Your faith is shown as you believe in Abba Father's promises. The Israelites grumbled and did not believe that Abba would keep his word to take them to a promised land. Instead, they accused him of trying to kill them (see Numbers 14:3). They complained about the way Abba was leading them through the desert. The Israelites did not honor Abba, nor did they humbly present their requests to him (see Exodus 17:3).

It is okay to be honest with Abba and present our requests and our worries to him. Then we move to believe his word to us and believe that he has our good in mind. We set our hearts to hope in what Abba Father has said and look past our circumstances to the promise that we cannot see yet. Faith is being convinced of the promise that we cannot see, so take hold of hope and believe! Abba Father is so pleased when we trust in him and trust in his promises.

Your faith is precious, as we see in 1 Peter 1:7: "So that the proof of your faith, being more precious than gold which is perishable, even though tested by fire, may be found to result in praise and glory and honor at the revelation of Jesus Christ."

Our faith is more precious to Abba Father than gold? Wow. I think it's easy to count gold as the best thing—if I had a lot of gold, I'd think of all the good I could do! But Abba counts our faith as the best thing. Seeing our faith and trust in him is a big deal. He is so honored when we trust in him and believe his word to us. Our job is to believe in Abba's promises to us. He will heal our hearts and restore our lives. Our faith will result in praise and glory and honor to Abba Father.

Remember, Abba's word is sure. Isaiah 55:11 says, "So will My word be which goes forth from My mouth; it will not return to Me empty, without accomplishing what I desire, and without succeeding in the matter for which I sent it." It is guaranteed that Abba will keep His promises. What he says will be accomplished. We can put our hope in Abba's word, which he gives us in Scripture and to our hearts directly.

Abba Father is your restorer.

ACTIVATION

Abba Father says he will be found by you. Jeremiah 29:13 says, "You will seek Me and find Me." Orient your heart around this truth: that Abba will not make it hard for you to meet with him. Instead, Abba truly wants to connect with you and restore you.

Keep this in mind as you progress through this activation. Chapter 6 will focus on Psalm 23 and our future. Psalm 23 is familiar to most of us, but I encourage you to read it with fresh eyes. In this next Recharge section make room for Abba to highlight things to you. Write down what you sense he is saying to you. You can spend as many days as you want recharging with Abba and reading Psalm 23 before reading Chapter 6. Again, we will also read Psalm 126 since this is our anchor promise. Abba is so good.

RECHARGE WITH ABBA FATHER

Total time: 10–15 minutes

Minutes 1–3: Silence and Reflection

Spend with a few minutes sitting with Abba. To begin, recite the phrase from Psalm 46:10, "Be still and know that I am God." Shorten the phrase each time to set your heart. Notice the nuances of shortening the phrase:

> *Be still and know that I am God.*
> *Be still and know that I am.*

Be still and know.
Be still.
Be.

For the remainder of the three minutes, sit in silence with Abba Father and just be with him. At the end, write down anything you have seen, sensed, or heard spoken to you. Know that it is okay and normal if you do not see or sense or hear anything. Abba enjoys simply being with you.

Minutes 3–5: Reading

Read Psalm 126; then read Psalm 23.

Minutes 5–8: Journaling

Write down any verses from these psalms Abba Father has highlighted and their meaning to you. This will allow you to remember what Abba has spoken to your heart.

Minutes 8–10: Sitting with Abba

End your time by spending two minutes in silence with Abba Father. At the end, write down anything you have seen, sensed, or heard spoken to you.

Throughout your day:

Worship songs: "Song of Heaven" by Mack Brock, "The Best is Yet To Come" by Mack Brock, "God of Breakthrough" by Mack Brock, "Time and Time Again" by Mack Brock

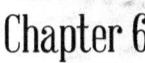

Chapter 6

The Future

Psalm 23

¹ The LORD is my shepherd,
I shall not want.
² He makes me lie down in green pastures;
He leads me beside quiet waters.
³ He restores my soul;
He guides me in the paths of righteousness
For His name's sake.
⁴ Even though I walk through the valley of
the shadow of death,
I fear no evil, for You are with me;
Your rod and Your staff, they comfort me.
⁵ You prepare a table before me in the presence
of my enemies;
You have anointed my head with oil;

My cup overflows.
[6] Surely goodness and lovingkindness will
follow me all the days of my life,
And I will dwell in the house of the LORD
forever.

In the beginning of the book, we saw that we can count on Abba Father's promises and that he is on our side, full of love and compassion toward us. In the last three chapters, we have learned that Abba Father fights our battles and protects us, that he has a plan for us and sees us, and that he is the faithful God who restores our life back to wholeness and reawakens our dreams. The more we see Abba's faithfulness, the more we can begin to trust him with our future.

Abba has a good future for you. Not only does he have a good future for you, but he is present with you now and has been with you in your past. We are learning who Abba is and how he thinks. We are also learning to see his activity in our lives.

The book of Hebrews shows us that Jesus trusted Abba through the pain all the way to his victory and became our example of faith in Abba. From the beginning of our faith to the end of our lives, we should be "fixing our eyes on Jesus, the author and perfecter of [our] faith, who for the joy set before Him endured the cross, despising the shame, and has sat down at the right hand of the throne of God" (Hebrews 12:2).

Abba Father was present with Jesus and showed Jesus the joy he would have on the other side of the cross. Abba Father is also present with us in our faith and will be with us to the end of our lives. He gives us promises we can look to with joy, just like he did for Jesus. Abba Father is our creator and wants to walk with us through the different stages of our lives. We will see that Abba Father is with us from the very beginning of our story, leads us and provides for us through the middle of our story, and has a wonderful ending to our story.

ABBA FATHER AT THE BEGINNING OF YOUR STORY

> The LORD is my shepherd,
> I shall not want.
> He makes me lie down in green pastures;
> He leads me beside quiet waters.
> He restores my soul;
> He guides me in the paths of righteousness
> For His name's sake.
> Even though I walk through the valley of the
> shadow of death,
> I fear no evil, for You are with me;
> Your rod and Your staff, they comfort me.
> (Psalm 23:1–4)

Abba Father is so good to us. We are not alone. I say that a lot because it is such a foundational truth. Abba Father has been with you from the beginning of your story. Abba does not just start you on your path and then see what happens; he walks with you and makes provisions for you. Abba is excited about you and your story. He sees both the beginning and the end of your story, and he has a plan to get you to the magnificent end. Our job is to have faith in Abba and believe what he says. Psalm 23:1 says Abba is our Good Shepherd and will provide everything we need, which includes physical needs and wants. Compare this with two other sayings of Jesus:

> "Ask and it will be given to you; seek, and you will find; knock, and it will be opened to you." (Matthew 7:7)
> "If you abide in Me, and My words abide in you, ask whatever you wish, and it will be done for you." (John 15:7)

Abba Father is inviting you to believe him and ask him. He is your Good Shepherd. You can be confident asking Abba for things because he wants to provide what you need and want. Abba is with you, and he is caring for you personally.

Verse two says Abba Father will lead you and give you rest in green pastures. You will get better at leaning into this rest that he has provided for you as you practice resting. He will also lead you to water that refreshes and quiets you.

When I got back into reading my Bible after my third child was born, I remember that it felt like I was drinking the most delicious water. I was being revived as I spent time with Abba in his Word. As you spend time with Abba, he will refresh you with water and quiet the storms in your heart. You feel quiet instead of anxious because you believe Abba is who he says he is, and you believe he is faithful.

My favorite line in these verses is in verse three: "He restores my soul." I am so thankful that Abba cares for my soul and restores me to how he designed me. I lean into this daily. If I'm feeling disappointed and sad, I make time to sit quietly with Abba to let him minister to me. Abba's perspective is much different from mine. I partner with Abba's perspective and let go of my old perspective. When I let him minister to me, I begin to feel joy and contentment. I rest in the knowledge that I can trust Abba and his plans.

Verse three also says Abba will guide me through my training in righteousness. In my own life, this looks like God showing me books that I need to read or songs I need to hear. He highlights Scripture in new ways that I can understand. There are times when I open my Bible to a book that I don't usually read. When I decide to read some of these verses, I find that Abba ministers to me in ways I wasn't expecting. All of this lets me get to know Abba as the Good Shepherd.

Psalm 23:4 says, "Even though I walk through the valley of the shadow of death, I fear no evil, for You are with me; Your rod and Your staff, they comfort me." Even when your training path goes through a bad valley, you can walk confidently knowing that Abba is with you and the Enemy is no match for him. You can walk with no fear! Your confidence comes from Abba's rod and staff which comfort you and direct you. For me, knowing Scripture has been an essential "rod and staff" that keeps me on Abba's path and prevents me from "jumping ship" to find what I think would be an easier path.

Another "rod and staff" for me is the ability to recognize fear. When I see that I am reacting in fear or feeling afraid, I know this is not Abba's path. I renounce fear and command it to leave me in the name of Jesus. Then I invite Abba to fill me with his peace and to show me the way to go.

Trust in Abba is a third "rod and staff" for me. In my life, if I come upon a closed door, I have learned that Abba is still with me. He will open the door or he will lead me somewhere else. I don't need to worry about missing something, because Abba is with me.

Throughout my life, whenever I have pictured the "valley of the shadow of death," I have pictured high, jagged walls of rock with a small path at the bottom. It is not a pleasant picture. One day, Abba changed my picture. The jagged walls of rock fell away, and I found myself in a great valley with lots of space. There were mountains in the distance on each side. He was with me. Even here, in this valley of the shadow of death, there were green pastures and still waters for me. This new picture has made it easier for me to believe in Abba and to trust in his plans for me.

What a wonderful Father we have. We can come to him daily to this place of green pastures, still waters, and restoration. We need a daily recalibration back to Abba Father's point of view, and he has provided this for us. Abba Father is the author of your story.

ABBA FATHER IN THE MIDDLE OF YOUR STORY

> You prepare a table before me in the presence
> of my enemies;
> You have anointed my head with oil;
> My cup overflows. (Psalm 23:5)

For me, as I have walked my path, I have often felt alone. For a time, my family lived far from people, and I didn't have many friends. There were people in my life who were judgmental toward me, so I felt I had no one to talk to about my marriage or my children or myself. This verse shows Abba's intentionality to be present in the middle of what we are going through. We are not alone. The verse acknowledges that we will have trouble, but that Abba will be there with us, protecting us and providing for us.

In the past, whenever I read this verse, the only thing I heard was that there were lots of enemies surrounding me. It was very unnerving. As I journeyed with Abba, he taught me that he was present with me, and I did not need to fear because he was looking out for me. Now I know that Jesus has disarmed and defeated the Enemy through his death and resurrection. The Enemy has been beaten by Abba Father. Let's settle this fact in our hearts right now. The Enemy is not stronger than Abba—the Enemy is not even equal to Abba! Abba Father is powerful. He is with you and loves you. Abba Father is present in the middle of your story. Invite Abba into your areas of dysfunction, and the Enemy will have to flee. Every day, invite the Holy Spirit to fill your home. Every day, sit with Abba and allow him to help you release offenses in your heart and forgive others. Every day, trust that Abba cares for you and wants you to be healthy. He knows what will minister to your heart. These are some of the things he "prepares on the table" before you.

I try to pay attention to my emotions because they often give me a clue to what I need at the moment. One night, I woke up in the middle of the night feeling intense sadness. It was overwhelming. As I was feeling stuck in the emotion, I realized that I was sad about my last child leaving for college, which was still two months away. It had not happened yet, but I was feeling sad about the future. Since I was half awake, it felt like a struggle to get my mind to interact with Abba, but I was able to ask Abba for help and find my bearings in his truths. The truths Abba brought me were that he had good planned for my future and would be with me. Abba helped me orient my mind and heart with hope and peace, and the sadness left me since it was a fabrication. I was able to go back to sleep in peace. My last child did leave for college eventually, and it was a happy occasion for me. I am so thankful for Abba's presence and his peace as I walk each day.

Whatever you need is what Abba provides on your table. Verse five says he also anoints you from your head to your feet with blessing, and his goodness will overflow you. This phrase "my cup overflows" is an analogy for your life. The picture is not of one tiny cup that Abba has accidentally poured too much into. Rather, your life is the cup, and Abba Father's goodness is abundant and overflowing into your life. You can orient your heart to notice Abba's goodness to you. It takes practice to believe in Abba and his goodness to you. Once you begin to see God as Abba Father and attribute the goodness in your life to him, you will be stunned by all the ways he cares for you. Then you will be able to let his goodness overflow out of you and into others.

This table that Abba Father sets up for you is for you and him together. He is the one preparing the table for you. Picture this: Abba is sitting with you at this table. He is smiling and laughing with you. The fellowship is sweet. The Enemy is null and void because of the presence of Abba Father. Then Abba Father anoints you from head to toe, and you feel the overflow of his blessings. It is so much that it just overflows. You are happy and you feel cared for.

You get to do this daily. You get to rest in Abba's provision for you and have Abba minister to you and be refreshed. You get to walk with Abba Father in his anointing and let it flow into others. It is so good and so fun! Abba Father is the author of your story.

ABBA FATHER AT THE END OF YOUR STORY

> Surely goodness and lovingkindness will
> follow me all the days of my life,
> And I will dwell in the house of the LORD
> forever. (Psalm 23:6)

We can count on Abba Father to be with us all the days of our lives until the end. The end of our life is the day we die, and Abba Father will definitely be with us at the end of our life and on into eternity. But I wonder if we tend to think that Abba's provision for us will stop at some point, as if we have used up our portion. The good news is that Abba never runs out of love for us or whatever else we need.

I find that Psalm 23:6 highlights five truths:

- We can rest in Abba's care for us while we are on this earth.
- There is no end to Abba Father's goodness to us.

WALKING WITH ABBA FATHER

- There is no end to Abba Father's loving-kindness and mercy to us.
- There is no end to Abba Father's presence with us.
- Abba Father will be with us to the end and beyond.

Wow! Amazing! Abba Father will be with us every day with his love and goodness and loving-kindness for us. He will walk with us through everything and still be with us at the end of our stories. We can rest in these truths and not worry. As we journey through our lives, we must remind ourselves that Abba is faithful and will not give up on us. Abba will finish what he has started because he loves us.

Philippians 1:6 shows us this: "For I am confident of this very thing, that He who began a good work in you will perfect it until the day of Christ Jesus." Abba will finish what he is doing in and for you. Our part is to believe that Abba is with us and full of goodness and loving-kindness to us. When we spend time with Abba, we allow ourselves to hear His loving messages. He loves us and will only speak loving messages to us, even when he is correcting a mistake. Having this relationship with Abba is the great prize we are seeking for.

Faith is believing in what Abba has said. Faith is seeing what Abba has promised even before it appears in our reality. Faith pleases Abba Father. As a reminder, Hebrews 11:1–2 tells us, "Now faith is the assurance of things hoped for, the conviction of things not seen. For by it the men of old gained approval." Our faith is shown as we believe in Abba and what he has said to us. Believing is the key to being able to rest in his care for us. Resting in Abba's care is a different way of believing. The idea of resting in Abba's care for us is similar to the idea of trusting that Abba will care for us well. We rest as we lean on Abba Father and trust in him.

The book of Hebrews contrasts *hearing* good news with *believing* good news and compares us with the Old Testament Israelites:

> For indeed we have had good news preached to us, just as the Israelites also; but the word they heard did not profit them, because it was not united by faith in those who heard. For we who have believed enter His rest, just as He has said, "As I swore in My wrath, they shall not enter My rest," although His works were finished from the foundation of the world. (Hebrews 4:2–3)

God's promise was that he would rescue the Israelites from Egypt and take them to live in the promised land, but they did not have faith or believe. The Israelites refused to go into the promised land, so they didn't get to obtain their promise; they didn't get to rest in God's care for them.

Abba is offering us his rest, which means we don't need to worry about how he will fulfill his promises to us. We can rest. He makes a way for us to hear the good news—the promise—and to believe it is true. Faith in Abba results in rest within our hearts. If we believe in Abba's word to us, we will enter his rest. If we hear Abba's word to us but don't believe it, we miss out on rest and become worried and upset. Rest means that we are allowing Abba to orchestrate the details, and we are not trying to influence the outcome.

When we are at rest, we are at peace and have confidence in Abba's ability to care for what concerns us. Rest does not mean that we are doing nothing, but rather that we are doing what Abba Father has asked us to do.

Often, I try to plan things according to my idea of what is right. But when I get carried away, I can hear Abba Father calling me to rest and asking me to wait for his timing. I feel his peace when I let go of my agenda and wait for him and his timing. An example of this was when my husband needed a garage and a shop on the side of our house. This shop would have covered up one of our bedroom windows. I felt worried, but I could hear Abba Father speaking peace to my heart. So I asked him to find a way to save the window for me. Then I rested and waited without worrying, and Abba saved the window. He provided a building for my husband that was better that anything we could have built and not far from our home. I felt so special that Abba would save the window just for me, and the new building was a great blessing to my husband too.

The end of Hebrews 4:3 says, "although His works were finished from the foundation of the world." This is stunning. All of Abba's works and plans were finished at the foundation of the world. We can trust that Abba has a plan, and because of his goodness to us, we can trust that his plan is really good. When you have faith that Abba will be true to his word to you, your heart will feel at peace and at rest no matter what is happening around you. Abba is saying to you, "Believe. Keep believing. Don't look around at the waves and the circumstances. Keep your eyes on me." Rest is a state of your heart that has confidence in Abba's ability to finish what he has started in you. From Abba's perspective, his plan is done. This is amazing and wonderful. This is why Abba Father is full of joy. This is why being in Abba's presence is the fullness of joy. This is why the joy of the Lord is strength for us.

Abba will be with you till the end, and Abba will see his promises come to pass in your life. It is marvelous to know that you are not on your own. He is walking with you and cares about you. Abba Father will never leave you. You are his treasured son or daughter! Believe it!

Abba Father is the author of your story.

ACTIVATION

I hope that through these activations, you have connected with Abba Father. Connecting with his love for you is of primary importance. I hope you realize that he likes you and wants to talk with you. I hope you have learned that Abba Father has good planned for you and is with you. I hope you have gained a rhythm of spending time with Abba Father. If you continue making space to spend time with Abba in his Word, he will lead you and show you your next step. I have gained so much from memorizing and meditating on the six psalms that we have discussed. A good starting place could be to read these six psalms again with Abba and spend an amount of time on each one before moving to the next. As you read Scripture, especially the same thing over and over, it will become a part of you, and the Holy Spirit will be able to bring it back to you when you need it. As you reread sections of Scripture, you will begin to understand how the Scripture fits into your life.

I believe Abba will show you your next step. You have a living, dynamic relationship with Abba Father. The most important thing is to make room in your life to listen to and talk with Abba Father. That is how relationships are built: "O taste and see that the Lord is good; how blessed is the man who takes refuge in Him!" (Psalm 34:8).

Abba Father is so good.